DEATH
a love letter

Weston Charlesworth

GLASSSPIDERPUBLISHING

ISBN: 978-1-957917-26-9 (paperback)
ISBN: 978-1-957917-27-6 (e-book)
Library of Congress Control Number: 2023902077

Cover design by Judith S. Design & Creativity
www.judithsdesign.com
Published by Glass Spider Publishing
www.glassspiderpublishing.com

I dedicate this to you, the reader. This collection of poems is my attempt to share my experiences with Complex Post Traumatic Stress Disorder, the loss of family members, and severe depression. Sometimes the will to live is hard to find, but we can do it together. There isn't a magic switch where everything gets better. But if we put in the work and stay brave, things can and will get better. As hard as it is, and it is so damn hard sometimes, we can get through this. Asking for help isn't weakness; it's the ultimate strength. You and I are now connected in our universal experience. Let's choose from this moment on to make the decisions of the person we want to be, regardless of what has led us to this point. Sometimes we might need help. The resources below are totally anonymous and are there for you even if you aren't suicidal. You're a brilliant star shining in the universe; sometimes talking things out is all we need. Thank you for taking the time to share this experience with me.

Sincerely,
Weston

Crisis Text Line: Text BRAVE to 741741
National Suicide Prevention Lifeline:
(1-800-273-TALK)

Contents

You are sitting on a comfortable sofa. There is an old television in front of you. A glass of your favorite beverage nearby, and some snacks. The television turns on. A red curtain on the screen parts. Behold...

Preface

Here I lay broken before you. I can't promise you'll love what's in store. You may not love it at all. I wish I could positively say it was all my fault.

I'd like to thank anyone in my life that has given me pain, or joy most, as all great friends will eventually give you both. I think you'll enjoy it best with little context, though this must be said:

These are the stories of one who was nearly dead.

All we can do is strive. None of us make it out of here alive.

Laughter

It's okay to laugh; life is a comedy. Even when it drives us to our knees. Sometimes it's so savage it's almost hard to believe. Is this show funny, or tragic? What is it exactly that you need? What's the purpose of this service that I've provided for you? Will it help you discover your universal truth?

Can it please just be love and joy that you are after? The program director is starting to squeeze out tears, I'm hoping from laughter. What's the purpose of this lust of dark disaster?

Maybe I'll end up on a podcast, then the story would be faster. We can just revel in the high points by a soothing-voiced broadcaster.

Perspective is an illusion self-manifested. One man's mountain of sorrow once divested could then be pressed into service and mined.

That is this poetry's purpose. This is a work of my newly found mind. Enjoy. And let's discover what I find.

Monsoon

They say when it rains it pours, but this feels
more like a monsoon. I keep running around
yelling to the sky that I'm barely staying alive.
An alien buffoon, trying to focus on the moon
through acid rain.

Focusing on one thing to ignore all the pain
caused by my brain. Constantly enflamed by
memories of pain, loss, and anger. Feelings of
love pass by like a stranger in the night. It's a sick
twist of fate that to heal, I must relive my plight.
That was so strong it shattered me in the first
stage. Like shaking a puzzle until everything fits
perfectly into its place.

The water is to my neck. I'm trying my best to
keep the memories at rest. Otherwise, they'll rise
in a torrent, to crush me in the strongest
memory's current; historical, dramatic, comedic,
or current event.

The mirages and visions are plentiful.
Demanding I stand as sentinel, reevaluating the
sentimental, realizing it was all a bait and switch.

They weren't trying to make you stronger; it was
a different situation completely. This is the bit
that deceives me.

Enter an emotional vampire begging for
sufferance for sins past committed.
Responsibility was, of course, omitted. How can
one allow one's mother to live on the streets? It
pled to me.

For ten months I slaved through every shiny
thing they had encountered in their life. This
snow scraper? There are only nine. What a
glorious find in this mine full of useless trash,
whose value is always slightly out of grasp, but it
could be worth something someday.

That day nears, and it's clear. What is left must
go to the dump. For weeks I'd been threatened
that I was driving them nuts, past the edge of
suicide. Often finding their things they would
hide only to be moved again another time, or ten.

One must not forget the ghosts, or the suicide
note they saved. The government watching, or
the neighborhood grave robbers. All putting a
stopper on any momentum to actually having

the opportunity to do what they confessed as dreams. This amidst the screams of "FUCK YOU!" when you politely explain the truth.

They signed a contract that would give them more money than they could ever find. In fact we should feel guilty for the people that bought it. Now my memories are all haunted with a dozen glorious friends helping us make it through the end.

As they spend eight hours sorting through spiders and dirt. Hoarded within the vampire's nest of shit everyone else would throw out. Listening as Kreacher roams their old home claiming the value of 90s magazines that don't care to be seen.

Sixteen-hour days being screamed at as you're reminded of childhood memories once buried. If this deal falls through, she's living with the fairies near the stream. She's incapable of this realization, so it falls on my shoulders to drag her kicking and screaming across the finish line. To what she professes is her dream.

If it doesn't pan out, it's my fault. The knife has twisted a gaping hole in the vault of my sense of self so deep. I don't know where to start. I am the result of a cycle of generational abuse, drowning in genetic self-hatred. To break it, I'm forced to be the patron of mental health professionals. Documenting in their confessionals that I don't always know what is real, or how to feel.

I don't know if I have the strength to paddle much longer, but I do have the courage to be consumed by the depths of trauma. If that's what's needed to go on and weather this monsoon.

Oh, to Be Content

Though night has come, and you've gone away,
at times though darkest the light does inside
shine. With a boom and a flash, my heart does
sway. A glimmer, a connection. I recall once
peace was mine.

The too-warm night brings naught but the frigid
cold, and a taste already grown muddled and
stale. A flickering heartbeat I'm graced to hold.
My lungs are filled with your light. I'm afraid of
the impending exhale.

Like metal too changed with water's harsh
mentality, I long for passion's true heat, billowed
not blown. I fear I grow brittle and frail. The
relentless shifts and swings to emotion's duality.

A word so small and immense. I would be
content. Instead, I lay beaten by fate's wanton
frivolity. Despite all of honor's best intent. I must
settle for that which torments me, a glimpse and
a memory, nothing more. Before I too am
welcome to a distant shore. I long to hold it again
where it need not be stored.

Thou oft pledged and never embraced. I must remember that this too shall pass. One must strive to the last, in the teeth of fate.
The challenge placed before all of man.

Oh, to be content again.

Invisible

With a flash and a glimmer, the world does shimmer. Sound is distant, control resistant. The tunnel comes, the funnel grows, Existence presents its square uncaring toes where the forgotten go.

Calling and urging, a cosmic yearning, how can I resist? No matter the tactic the vacuum persists. I must resist, for the universal purpose I must exist.

Whether I step forward tall and bold or shamble in a fog induced by systems bought and sold. I'll strive for the existential goal.

I am alive, I will survive and someday I will thrive. Claim your victories of joy and bliss, for at times it's the entirety of your wish. To sit calmly in the moment and feel this. The improbable universe finding its purpose.

Third Muse

I don't mean to confuse; there's a reason for the
bruising. The all-consuming silence, the squeal of
bike tires, and the inhalation of collective breaths.
"These two are surely about to be dead." He
didn't even tap his brakes. The crosswalk clearly
states we had sixteen seconds more right of way.

We just wanted to go see a Modest Mouse show,
something I'd been chasing for ten years or more.
Out for a nice night after my brother died and
mother cried it was all my fault. I wish he
would've been driving a Renault. Instead, we
careened into the side of a black Dodge Nitro.

He didn't start braking until he was through the
entire intersection. Spinning on the pavement,
I'm looking for direction from a dozen strangers
arranging around us saying we almost died.
Then ensuring we were actually alive. They
knew right away we wouldn't be fine.

They call for an ambulance when one is right
behind them; we were a hundred yards from the
bike valet. It was quite the conundrum of reason

as they are pleading for me to stay on the ground. As I point out that they could just turn around and shout.

The police finally arrive and ask if I'm fine, or if I need an ambulance. Ah, America, the land of the free—just not our healthcare. I've nearly died while looking at my wife. We both decide we can survive this calamitous experience without a ten-thousand-dollar taxi ride. Not because we don't need one, but because we aren't sure if we want to pay the egregious bill.

I ask the cop if this will impact our insurance. He shrugs and says he can't see why it will.

I get up off the ground, grateful I'm alive as I stare down at the handlebars and the reversed front tire. My wife hit her head so hard the lenses of her glasses popped out. The policeman is more worried about the local traffic route.

We move off to the corner of the intersection. The police barely talk to us again. We are just another call on the radio. They don't care that my sanity just ended.

The driver was sorry for what he had done; he was just too busy looking at his thumb as he tried to book another delivery. Now if anything unexpected pops up on my right side I start shivering and my skin turns aflame. All because I wanted to go see a concert for my birthday.

The rules clearly state "three strikes, you're out." I just didn't know they meant my mind. This is when I decide that I must put this terrible experience to use. This time, I'll use trauma as my muse.

Confidence

I have the confidence of a pinwheel in a hurricane. Screaming and soaring in a torrent constantly on edge of obstruction and destruction.

Like a base jumper, sans chute I plummet, praying for a soft landing. Grasping my soles with my toes and hoping those are shoals not coral I'm headed for.

Hello, I am Joe's brother. I'm calling to find out how he died. A pause, a deep sigh. We don't know. He died alone. That means we have to treat it as a homicide.

Does that mean...
We don't think it was suicide.
How did he seem?
Surprised.

Upon impact, my soul is cast back behind stacks of memories. I then exist in the periphery. Questing to return to where I am me. While my mind struggles to keep me alive.

Grief

How cruel is it? To miss that which is forever
gone. That joyous minstrel of that which we
know belongs.

A caterwauling of reality's sadness, a naked light
bulb is all that hides my terror, all that preserves
my fastness.

A flick of a switch exposes my breastplate as less
steel than tin. Images of opportunities lost
masticate all that which is within.

A cacophony of memories storm forth, some full
and others shorn. Foresworn, and often unborn
to the light of day. This is my heart's dismay.

Yet, one can never forget there will always be
tomorrow's dawn. And all that glitters is not yet
gone.

Sunrise

The patter of your best friend's footsteps and the sound of your breath. It's where I find myself when I can't seem to rest. A half-drunk coffee sitting on the cold stone. It's just me and Poppy, and we are all alone.

The jagged silhouette eases into view from black to blue, patches of trees backed by that amber hue. Fall is here and the air is biting; an old cow fence emerges as the sky is brightening.

A tumble of stones makes a raucous sound; Poppy's ears poke out from around the mound of broken sandstone, or maybe it's granite and blue. It's hard to tell until the light shines through.

Today, it's me and my dog searching for something old; the bite of the air makes my fingers cold.

On the lookout for joy everlasting, on the way up, Dolly was blasting. This isn't an island in the stream, but it's not far off.

The ruddy red sky will soon be lost. Pangs of hunger ring true with a loud harangue—looking at Poppy, she's thinking the same thing.

When you can't sleep and there's nothing to do, sometimes it's best to go see the sky change from black to blue.

Joy Hangover

My dopamine and serotonin are boning. I want to taste purple, hit it. We're going. One eight seven bad vibes, when the tone hits just start rowing.

Journey through the bushes, today's song is yet to be sung. Gaze at blades of grass or create the next Aqualung.

If those talents elude you, it's okay! WE WILL GET THROUGH TO YOU! Stand up, sit down, plant your toes. Strive to impress your dog. See where true love goes.

If the situation seems dire, think off the cuff. *Numquam obliviscar!* YOU ARE ENOUGH!

Note

I was strong enough for the number, but not the
note of your eternal slumber.

Why is it so hard to delete a file of someone you
miss? Despite every time your eyes graze the
title, your heart starts to hiss.

Is it the fear that you'll somehow forget? This
person, who you can't offset for even a moment.

Maybe it's just the fear of love's labor lost and
admitting the ultimate cost of life's finality. Then
again, sometimes I question my own sanity.
It's probably just vanity.

There is a certain mystique to a poet's descent
into the madness of antiquity. It lacks the
ambiguity of modernity's pretentious fluff.

Fidelis ad Urnam

Loyal to the grave: A universal truth, or its
opposite and the enemy of all proof? To believe
is to animate, yet mine is an impression more
dour than great.

An eclipse: Does it reveal proof of the outside
cosmos? Or strike out the light of heaven-sent
truth? Are we meant to see outside our self-
imposed chains or to ignore such grand beauty to
have the same?

One you hurl through at a glacial place,
bounding and breaking.
Or is it faking?
To live?
Or to expand in stasis?
Comedy and drama are but one of many faces.

Torment: To jump and see? To breathe? Even if
it's just a moment to be free of choice's misery. A
man in love with virtue's glamour, or its inverse,
the very measure of lust? Is it fate enamored, or
do I see a chink in its rust?

A virtue so profound and honored, to question it
is insanity. Or is that too a choice of vanity? To
know thyself, or to trust history's ledger?

Which leap is faith?
And which to the dredgers?
Another folly idea strewn among the pebbles.

How can my heart fight to find that which is
right? Not just now, but nearly every night?

Dirty Pass

Who's this stranger in the mirror?
It couldn't be clearer that you're not steering.
You're clutching at straws trying to force
meaning.

It's just flashbacks and backward hats, sitting on
the floor watching her drink another Diet Coke.
You don't know what's coming, in the future
you're so fucking broke.

It comes back in a flash of tears, all those lost
years. I tapped because I was scared and was
only half aware.

The future may not be set, but you can't go back
and fix all your regrets.
I'm supposed to just pick up and go on now?
Like everything is fine?

That field is plowed. That's water, not wine.
Why does it feel so good remembering the
season of snow, and our time?

The lives in my head seem so clear. I don't know if it's the whiskey or all that beer. But at least I can steer and be free to imagine what it would be like if I was actually me.

Why do I drive these roads looking for ghosts? They've moved on. Why can't I?

Just another day spent searching for hope. Trying to find some other way to cope with choosing the easy way.

Now I spend all day inventing something to say that will somehow make everything okay.

Acceptance

Maybe we don't need to understand everything,
and we need to accept more. Sometimes the
answer is blunt and short.

We forget that a castle is made of broken stones,
a mountain's shattered bones. Piled up this way
and that, this grand façade, no more than a
cliffside's hat.

To understand can often be to dissect, yet
acceptance is where true love is met. Not with a
desire for others to change but like that castle, we
can be pieces simply arranged.

So as time brings its gusty deluge, our hearts are
less exposed. Gazing through the storm at distant
shores. Our armor protecting that which we can't
lose.

I am the rock, oft found on the ground.
Once a part of a mighty mount.
I've lost my moss as I am tossed about.
Content to be, no need to shout.

In search of a fortress big or small, I'd quite love to be a countryside wall. Gazing lazily back at the sun, to reminisce about my life's run.

To just be myself, that would be fun. A happy piece of scenery near some wood; accepted as I am. No need to be understood.

Sunset

It's just another Sunday, you've got much more
than a headache, and sad news. You're eating
breakfast at noon in your hometown greasy
spoon. You don't know a single soul in the room.
Everyone around you is paying for their crimes,
last night's mistakes or another lifetime's.

You can see it every night, the shadow of the
door. Your keys thrown beside you. Shattered
and broken on the floor. You don't know if it's
innocence lost or stolen; your brain throbs as
though it's misspoken with too many regrets
slammed into this tiny-ass closet. Last night you
added another one, and today you've damn near
lost it.

As you stare into the middling distance, you
remember that old phrase, "Thou shalt do no
harm." With a dull ache and the taste of cold
coffee, you sometimes want to cut your arms.
Ghosts of all these aches make your body start to
shake. As you try and process another damn
shame. Sometimes you remember more than just
a name.

All any of us want is to have a good time, but somehow, somewhere you've crossed that thin line. These undercooked eggs are as broken as your mind. You focus back on your plate and try to return to the moment; the frustration builds as you can't seem to own it.

In a muddled haze and a creeping chill, you must convince yourself this moment is really real. Not again with this old pain—you can feel the tremors coming in again. Is the world shaking, or is it just me eating stale toast and trying to breathe?

You sprint to take a piss so everyone will miss the sound of your shamefaced breakdown.

Staring in the mirror, it couldn't be any clearer that the person looking back isn't you.

Barely even moving but the heart is really choosing to run up something steep.

You think, "Maybe I'm just dying; my soul is really diving somewhere deep. I can't even see me. All of my senses are reeling. Someone call the hearse."

You hope you can find some ending; the colors just stopped blending. Somehow this is so much worse.

"I hoped this would fade with time, but I'm longing for what once was mine. A sense of some grander thirst."

Each day brings it further. You don't know if it's absurd, or if you can sense if this is a memory or the first time it's happened, still the chills are fully wrapping up your chest. You just want to forget.

...but not that just quite yet.

Before each new dawn, there always is a song of a sunset.

Final Moment

Is the universe listening? Or just witnessing my
fall? I thought my foundations stone but
apparently, it's just straw. Feet dangling and
twisting in the wind, is this a new beginning or a
comedic end? Staring at a strange ceiling
searching for new meaning of a life on the mend.

All the tingles and stabs of these nerves all on
fire. My vision singles and grabs, lashing to these
tires. Rambling and shaking down this tunneled
road. Is that the earth quaking or just me?
Ambling, it's taking this funneled soul. I'm
rattling around so hard I can barely see.

Life seems to be one big trigger warning; I
struggle to make it through each morning. I don't
know what's worse: dreaming or being awake.
Sometimes it's almost too much to take.

Hometown Lycanthrope

Lost on the morning's mist, the fresh scent of
memories missed. Coverings torn asunder, last
night you fought for your life. Red marks on
your throat, raised fresh from the fight.

You wander your usual routes trying to restore
your mind. The marks aren't all unkind as you
find an empty Trojan packet. Maybe you can
bring her to your front-porched casket.

Life moves on and so must you, but the cure is
far from proven. The next harvest moon is nearly
glooming, you can feel it in your veins, the blood
lust booming.

As you see the luminance over the mountains,
your skin boils like a fountain. Your breath
catches and you can hear the shouting. Your
heart starts pounding. In a flash, a memory is
surrounding.

This curse from a single night's bite. Somehow is
chasing you your whole life. You try a new path
and feel fate's wrath. You look east and the pull

is so vast. How many times do you have this
same thought? What is this curse that reminds of
what you lost?

You've tried silver bullets and black labels.
Genres innumerable state the cure is a fable. You
long in your marrow to stop this lust so feral. I
long for biting frost and broken thumbs, and life
less sterile. Am I chasing crumbs as I put all in
peril?

Often these feelings bring more than can be
wrote; the old me is lost in this cursed haze.
Losing track of so many days. Am I cursed to be
the hometown lycanthrope?

A Carny's Tale

It's a yarn as old as time, or so I thought.
Working for a living so the house isn't lost. It
starts at six in the morning around the end of
May, when you start to work while others dream
of play. The tent goes up and the clown comes
out, the back of an '84 station wagon with a
Buick badge for a mouth.

You're trying not to starve but to others it's a
joke; this is your first job. But it's your dad's
fourth. It's not what others think, being carny
folk.

In this town, it starts with a parade in celebration
of their random fruit's day. They may see a car
show or get a painting on their face. But that's
not for you; you're too busy raising rent to pay.

Your family will make $700 if you've got some
luck. Seems like a lot until you have to pay the
man in the city truck. He smiles and waves as he
takes their cut—it's a whole lot of effort to keep
working in this hut.

Margins are slim when everybody but you wins,
especially when it means it all goes back into
your mom's latest scheme. All for a plate of food
that's at best tepid, just to support Mom chasing
another pyramid. If she can just sign up another
four, she might make district manager. If not
now, maybe next calendar.

If we just work hard enough, it will all pay off.
And like that, my childhood was lost.

It Cuts Deep

It cuts deep and it shouldn't, that thing I wanted
but you wouldn't. Some things can't be taken
back, and it was a vicious attack. Because in you
I've placed my trust, the fact you couldn't even
muster the effort required to support my rare
bluster. So that my point cannot be missed. I
gave you the soul behind my kiss. That part for
you I did not resist.

An offering that for you there is nothing I
wouldn't do, yet you merely tried for a moment
or two. Tossed like a bad penny down to the curb
so that your life would not be disturbed.

Soft Robot

Whose idea was a supple machine? So easily
ruined, this capsule of my being. The
programming shorts and feels the weather;
couldn't God have come up with something
better? Why must I glitch when I stare at that
sunset remembering the feeling of your smile?
That most worthwhile of whiles. The crinkle in
your eyes creating my programming's demise.

The intelligent design seems missing in mine.
The most subtle lack of dopamine triggers
memories half seen. With a crackle and a tingle
the synapsis mingles, presenting memories
linked, not singled. If I just process these feelings
that have me continually reeling, will I reboot?
Living more astutely finding pleasure in my
daily duties? Does this coding need proving, or
can I simply begin moving on?

Anon, to a life reformed if not newly born. One
where I can function with a modicum of security
and an abundance of surety. To live, to dream,
and chase wonderous thought. Not just merely a
broken soft robot.

Unread

The meaning seems clear until you hold someone
dear. The chasm brings spasm of regret into the
rearview mirror.
Looking back, all I see is you, and I lose sight of
all else in front of me.
How is this the same life and the moments lay
wasted?
Every moment you walked away, I start chasing.

No matter how fast I hurry, the memories are
blurry.
That life is not one I've ever had.
I'm locked in this cell knowing what drives me
mad.

When listing regrets, some say they have none.
Is that because they always run?
Not away but forward to that which they adore?

Here comes another panic attack—eyes on the
road and the tingles set.
Flashes of shadows your periphery begets.
God damnit, the sun just set. Not just on your
past but the road in front of you.

The lights are blinding; the cold pierces straight
through you.

For the millionth time I glance at the screen, but I
know exactly what will be seen. It's so petty and
shitty knowing you're in a better place. Behind
that barrier of my terrestrial city. How I long for
that grace. There's so much that hasn't been said,
but that screen will always say unread.

Trust

How can I believe in that which has let me down
so many times before? Not gut nor heart but
brain and more. Evidence proves a decision's
regret; was it just the wrong criteria were met?
The yoke of choice weighs heavy on my soul—
what's that? How many more questions to go?
Staying or leaving, committing or grieving.
Every thought an action, even those that are
distractions. What must I do, and how can I
prove to know what is wrought of honest truth?
I've been conditioned to not trust that which I
see, to never know which feeling is truly me.
The ante is high, the bets are mounting. Is this
the right choice? The consequences move
mountains. It feels like a hurricane, but it's more
of a gust. I'm so immobilized by the trait I find
myself lacking: trust.

Savior

In the tornado of emotions that wrap around me,
the mention of your name makes me free. A
transcendental light nearly out of reach. To be
purified in your presence is all I seek. Ripping
me through the ethereal firmament of universal
life. Its breath going in deeply and then out. The
moment of creation, of love and eventual
devastation. Something worthy only of the
devout.

Not thrusting or cutting or floating and jumping,
but a yearning so strong and deep you feel
nothing and everything, stronger than gravity.
More vast than a broken atom's savagery. Each
moment you feel closer, it strengthens your pulse
as you rush to the pulsar. The righteous moment
of saving, but your resolve dissolves and your
lead is fading. A dirty white mist, your divinity
is erasing. You have to resist—one day, you'll
catch love's favor. Then you will be embraced by
your savior.

Quitting

I hate it so much, but I understand it so well.
Quitting is admitting you failed. Your spirit
broken and frail and knowing you can't put it all
back together.

A hooker, a cigarette lighter, and a box of
Kleenexes, it's all I need. Maybe in the morning
I'm going to know what I seek.

Sure, replace it with something else that you'll
quit on. What more must a person do?
I'm terrified of my rage, pouring out at myself.
Why can't I do better?
Will I quit on that, too?
Yeah, I've tried so hard to earn bliss.
Pretty fucked up I feel like this.
I've spent so much of my life trying to make
people love me.

I just want to love someone who loves me like I
love them.
It's as easy as it is to say that.
That phrase that constantly eludes my grasp.
That feeling that thrusts you into space.

Soaring through the cosmos of joy and light. Nothing gaudy, but a heavenly delight. Soaking in its glorious rays. I wish to reside in it the rest of my days.

Daydream Judgment

I wander back and forth. Should one not
daydream? To carry us through life's rough
discourse on imagined life's paving. Though
translucent and as soft as gossamer wings, it is
said one can occasionally dream them into being.

A life joyous, one of comfortable calm. To live a
life of support and self-belief is my psalm. Our
heartbeats are numbered; is it so bad to think of
slumber's thoughts during the day when
unencumbered?

To be thrifty with what is limited shouldn't
involve so much shifting or lifting of one's
spirits. To escape the fog of mere existence, that
is the fiercest resistance to my daily
reminiscence.

To lift my shoulders above my brain's clouds
into miniscule clearance. Why can't my brain
hold with fast adherence?

Joseph

The silence is deafening. I'm still reckoning with
the fact that you're gone. I'm used to your quiet,
but it still destroys me that you've moved on.
With a smile and a shrug, we all understood, you
had your own quiet way. Somehow, we usually
knew what you were trying to say.

You always knew how to give but never receive,
and as long as you lived you never tried to
deceive. You'd always show up with a gift, but
it's your missing smile that sends me adrift.

It's October 13th—you should've turned 44 today.
Two packs a day for 30 years took you away.
Your heart's the one thing I never thought would
quit. It was so big and caring and yet here I sit,
crushed with grief and mourning going through
a rolodex of memories you're in.
At least I can say I loved you as much in life as in
death. Happy birthday, my dearest brother
Joseph.

Boundaries

The give and take as we try and relate. Push too
far or not enough and it's a perilous fate. Human
connection is at stake. Crimes of unknown
punishment in place, as the edge of our
relationship is made. Some advances are
allowed, and others must be stayed.

Some, through attrition, are robbed of ambition.
I've spent so much time pushing the flood back
that I lack the ammunition required to feel love.
Like inhaling arsenic, my skin burns like an
arsonist. Often, it's exhausting to re-establish that
which vanished, with one action one must be
banished. Once these walls are smashed, they
can take twice as long to build back.

Work Trip

My skin's on fire without any desire. There
seems to be no solution to my latest evolution of
fate. Staring at a dark ceiling for…is it seven
hours, or eight? I seem to only feel what's inside,
not out. One second I'm dead inside, the next I'm
bursting like a fount.

Why can't these feelings end? I'm supposed to be
on the mend. I don't want to die, but right now
I'd prefer to be dead. There's got to be more to
life than being watered and fed. Fake it till you
make it or something like that, but there's no end
in sight, and the lack of improvement continually
distracts.

The circus proceeds as I stand aflame, sweating
like a dam is breaking. Clawing at my arms
trying to find change, but the feelings are the
same and the searing is making the shaking too
much to keep on faking. A passing thought of
calm comes as slowly as the dawn, rolling in like
a breath of fresh air. Inside, I stare at the fountain
of peace as the mountain starts to decrease.
Only two days left: rinse and repeat.

To Be

To be or not to be? That is, in fact, my question.
To toil through in search of some purity, or seek
a new bastion? In that purest of light risk being
charred asunder, or is that life's true blunder?
Will I be a pile of scorched detritus or rise like a
phoenix from life's ashes? That's the query: to
live in what fashion?

Is trying one's best enough when hearts are
involved? Is there a position more evolved, how
can I temper my heart with steel's resolve, not
brittle and frail but mendable to life's travails.

Delphi is no more; who in the universe can I
prevail upon? I need guidance to meet fate head
on. I just want joy. Is that too much to ask? Why
must it be such a task?

I've strived for hours unknown to find a life that
is glowing, one where being loved is surely
known. Yet the effort lays like a broken bottle
with juices flowing—strewn upon a dirty floor,
illuminated by sunrise through an open
bedraggled door.

Why must I be tormented by life's true meaning?
Searching for a purpose unseen so as not to hurt
those who have formed my being. Why is the
answer shadowed and unseen to life's true
query?

To be or not to be makes me so weary.

Yes, I Exist

Is existence enough? To be more than just
universal stuff? Am I caught drinking from a
trough of falsehoods? Am I too naive to want
more than lying that I am good?

Why am I not comforted by so many luxuries
about me? The more I learn, the more I strive to
be heard. The more I wish to shout that I stood.
Not sat in complacency and holding back those
around me.

It should be so easy to accept what I have, and
others could. I oft think they should. I wish to
grow, not sit about but to rove. To distant shores
and hear the misty roar of rivers yet unseen.
That, to me, is what living means.

To risk a fall from the heavens so I might find
more than that which I've been given. I wish not
for glory or fame, but to be living a life worthy of
having a name.

To be named is to be realized by the universe. A
cause so weighty and worthy that I should give

more than just the first heave of effort. To be more than just a good credit score.

Should I settle in the glories I have, or should I resist? To put it all on the line and do more than merely exist.

Starburst

Not just a sunrise, a revelation. A flash in the
grimmest desolation. To know pure truth and
reason for primordial creation. A glimmer in the
eye and your beautiful smile—for it a man would
walk a thousand miles. To swear on one's life,
the risk of sorrow and strife, and it would all
have worth.

Though it lasts but a minute, the fires burn
eternal, feelings not just carnal floating in my
sight only to be seen at mind's night. As strong
and warm as any sun's light. With the deepest
hunger, my soul does thirst for that which I
glimpsed first, as time has swelled and years
were felled. I still long for another time to feel
that starburst.

I never appreciated the care and the beauty. The
feeling of soul and heart's unity. Catacombed in
this emotional frost. My spirit sings for that
which is lost. The tiniest flicker and I'm stricken
with a vision of a new life. One where joy is
possible, without the crucible of constant fight.

Could life mean more than strife from our moments last to first? In my anesthetized state, I hope for a different universe. One where I can abide in that starburst.

I'm So Tired

It's not just in my eyes, this feeling that I find—
it's lifting this invisible weight, the effort in my
mind.

I can feel it in my chest and gut, this constant
wondering what, means what? All the things
that I didn't choose. I'm so exhausted of
moments that will haunt me, something I'll never
lose.

I just need to shut it all down.

Coming like an early spring, when as the world
sings. I'll come back above ground when the
world is filled with less anxious sounds.

I'm just so tired; I guess I'm not wired for all the
things that I must do.

I'll keep on grindin' even though I'm dying. I just
have too much that I want to prove.

It's grating, all this assimilating. How am I
supposed to know what to do?

I must adapt to the latest situation and all this conflict that I'm facing. Lord, I wish I could just have you.

That feeling of contentment, when my heart can just be set in a calm and wholesome groove.

I'm just so tired; I guess I'm not wired for all the things that I must do.

I'll just keep grindin' even though I'm dying. I just have too much that I need to prove.

The Longest Days

My breath strays from its regular pattern as once again I'm unwittingly battered. The smallest reaction to an interruption undoing the latest statement's construction.

A nail also has a point, but it does not join boards if it's wantonly bludgeoned with heinous blows. Twisting the nail grudgingly into the direction appointed with less accuracy than this prose.

Instructing to strike thus when it's already occurred. Is akin to being hit by a bus, for that would be preferred. If another pointless fight could be deterred.

I'm an empty silhouette, my soul crushed, battered, burnt, and beaten. Slayed, ripped, and carelessly eaten. Swallowed defecated and spat on. All to be built up and rationed.

To crush a man in a single blow is too easily done, something for the cheapest fun. No, it's better for all to be told of your love so bold. Then to publicly scold him for the audacity of saying he could do something that ended up being outside of his capacity.

While occasionally soft-spoken. I don't make gestures or tokens without thought and care. That you would think so gives me the utmost despair.

As my integrity degrades and my spirit decays, the minutes strained long and thin. Burning holes into my skin. I struggle to portray my essence on these longest days.

Self-Fulfilled Prophecy

Anxiety stands like a pariah on my chest.
I just want to do what's right and hope fate
handles the rest. Instead, it's a living death, of
seeing what I want and settling for what they say
is best.

Where is the line of fate's faithless and actions
chasteness?
To do enough but not too much.
Is something myself I cannot trust.
Reading the room, I've said too much—but deep
down not nearly enough.

With the timid grace of one narcissistically
raised. I don't seek praise but acknowledgment.
To be seen or heard, a small gesture, just a
platonic friend. Selling myself short for fear of a
catatonic end.

High hopes are never truly shattered.
All that matters is the deafening silence of loss.
The frigid cold of neglect's frost.
All created in my mind. In reality, everything is
probably fine.

Coiled so tight I struggle to unwind when
causing a loved one an imagined hard time.

It's not pessimistic to be realistic.
I try not to be dour, honestly;
it just feels like a self-soured prophecy.

Another Blow

I swear I looked. I tried to be prepared, and then
it came out of thin air. My world crashing down
around me. I swear it wasn't there.

I'm sick of fighting back, battered and broken.
It's more than just blood that flows. I need more
than just a token. I don't think I can deal with all
these memories once stowed.

A whisper feels like a hurricane. I'm leaning
against the wall waiting for another fall. They
say it's the impact that hurts, but they're lying.

It's hearing death's bawl. I can't fight what I can't
see. When I mention it, my heart stutters, my
hands shake, and I start to mutter. Looking for
the source yonder, it's just too much to ponder.

Right before impact—this massive dread, it's too
much to pretend. It's not living if you constantly
think tonight might be the end.

Semper Fi

Sometimes I get sick of telling everyone the lie,
that I don't want to die. We talk more seriously
about suicide than genocide. Yet expect those
most maimed to stand up and fight with a smile.
All the while the world is in denial about
scientific facts and presidential trials. People ask
what has given me the blues. I don't know, have
you turned on the fucking news?

It doesn't matter the channel, just watch the
talking heads scramble to ramble in front of a
backdrop with a camel. How can you trust
someone in sandals? Once I believed society had
at least some ability to critically think. Then I
found no one cares what school children drink. Is
that sugar and lead in your purple drink?

It doesn't matter how many facets are swarming
about the critical state of global warming. The
white fascists are charming. We should let
corporations do farming, with unregulated
workforces. Then weaponize the "capitalistsas"
fawning over fake armies of "Christians"
abhorring the teaching of Jesus, confusing them

for Marxists, imploring to be treated with dignity and respect. That would require someone not to be bereft of common sense. They'd rather let pregnant mothers rest in alleyways getting their comeuppance for not fighting back harder. Allowing the insurance companies and jailers to grow their swollen larders.

My apologies, it's my fault for caring, I of course should consider how the shareholders are faring. The trust-fund kids of course are the ones daring to take risks. As we argue if we should let children and the elderly get sick. All in honor of sacred profit in Q1.

You're right, I should just try and have more fun. While Elon Musk shoots a car into the sun and openly funds an oligarch's son's presidential run. Everything is going to be fine. The politicians are trying to only partially undermine the demise of that which so many soldiers gave their lives for.

We must be polite and respectful of our oppressors; we must always be aware that we are lesser. To be trite is what makes you an aggressor, but fuck my feelings, right?

Are we playing fifth-dimensional chess, or is it too late to tell? All of this on top of a personal hell caused by a guy delivering Taco Bell blowing a red light. Everything happens for a reason on a Tuesday night. If I want happiness, I just have to try. I just need to be more grateful and Semper Fi.

Obsession

It's best not to obsess over what we find in the
recesses of our mind.
The effects are reeling and unkind, chasing an
intoxicating feeling looking for a sign.
Sometimes what is…simply is.
And that's just fine.

All too often I am stressing, looking for some
miraculous blessing, visions of God's sending.
To allow my heart to stop rending with each
recurring session.
Another life lesson.
Looking for patience to allow feelings to lessen.

Not another great indiscretion, to wish and
dream of happenstance happiness is a most vile
regression.
Chasing euphoric delirium another anti-truth
serum.
In which I could spend seasons for the reason of
perceived joy.
Not lived but believed as if it was the very stones
I stand upon. Alone another victim of Troy.

With each breath, a mile passes staring through
battered rose-colored glasses.
At pasts with a different future, acting as some
kind of suture for my shattered soul. Its sole
purpose to somehow grow a sense of being.
Freeing me of this life's lesson, but not—that, too,
is an obsession.

Poetry

Is the self-flagellation of the imagination.
Merely the meter of sight or sound.
That somehow seems profound.
Describing one's surroundings of themselves or
their spirit.
It can lift the soul when you hear it.
Your inner demons quiver when they feel it.
It can only deceive if you do not believe.
Your emotion held deepest it can retrieve.
An internal tempest it seeks to relieve.
It allows us to walk tall and stoically.
This wonderful thing we call poetry.

Reflection

Who stands before me is as much myself as
Persephone. Cursed to be lured to Hell's door by
random chance and more. Behind me lay the
spoils of spilled seeds grown as weeds to
entangle my mind. If only deep sleep I could
find. Then some solace could betide, instead I
hang akimbo across my bedside, and my sanity
hangs in limbo of self-reflections it derides.

I wish I could say I hope you're happy now, but
honestly, I don't care. Even these words hold
only the stench of your miasma's air. The title of
mother is earned, your self-righteous demeanor
and imagined slights make my stomach churn.
You suck the life out of all around you, I regret
the moment my father ever found you.

How you raised your children had a cost, all but
one of us you've lost. One dead and one envious
of those memories tossed into oblivion. Instead, I
stand here as a tribute to death's call.
Mesmerized by the false sweetness of no
memories at all.

Misspoken Words

Like a slip in the night the current shifts, the
ripples sit right below the lips. A combination of
thoughts, the moment lost. As you said what
memory wrought not what you meant.

It floats on the breeze, this sterile moment of
unease. You see the reply stutter and cease, the
brain mutters and flaunts your intent, will mercy
be lent? Will there be release or will this moment
be burned into memory, and mind, for you later
to find? Empty bottle in hand as your spirit is
tried, staring at the closed blinds after another
day's grind.

Like a flood's torrent, you're eroded more than
you can warrant. Isn't it all a bit much? To miss a
one-ton vehicle only to have the whiff crush your
mind and soul? What was it the man said in the
stole? My guilt led to this role of peasant slave to
revelries pull.

To flounder in the boiling memories of joy and
bliss, only to realize it's the last cyst of love
missed. To be lanced and cleaned in this caustic

dream. Only reminds me of what you mean to me, meant to me, were heaven-sent for me. An unrivaled string on a tapestry of life and it seems future lost. At the ultimate cost.

A drip in a stream of flashes I must ford as I dream of life's narrative and bash it into a misbegotten story. And there again I seem to attribute meaning to what is seen only in forged memory. More effort than one can afford of a cautious chord, all musing inspired by a few misspoken words.

Alone

Sitting in a sterile room, one cleansed with a
mop, not a broom. Hearing only the heater roar,
as they pump air back where no light is stored.
I'm here for my seventh checkup, paying a
professional to confirm I'm messed up.

I lay forgotten and abandoned by chances both
random and prophetic. All is torn asunder, even
life domestic. What pain have I wrought? That I
focus only on that which is lost.

My senses are reeling as my soul hovers against
the ceiling, but my eyes are attached through the
back of my head. Am I dreaming? Or is this real
life instead?

Not all nightmares are filled with gore, some
have only banalities in store. Useless repetitions
to help a billionaire keep score. I've lost all of
that which I once adored, it lays out before me
like film on the floor.

Memories past, present, and lost futures. This
can't be healed with simple sutures. The day's

light burns holes in the fragile acetate, melting
and bonding at a frenetic pace. The more I worry
it, the more it agitates. It's a feeling too hard to
relate, to be sitting in this haunted state.

The best I can do is attempt to tame the tone, so I
don't maim the bone to my soul's home. Clawing
my toes, I try to caress the loam through my
shoe's foam. I'm just so sick of feeling alone.

Missing Yo

I miss our conversations, the dumb ones that made us laugh. The ridiculous notions living in our past. The crinkles by your eyes when casting that beautiful smile.

The room lights up, the pupils widening at the brush of touch. How calming and exciting! Hugs that lasted days and reading the latest craze. Brightening my wonderful gaze. Eyes dilating to drink in nirvana's blaze.

Shaking our heads at each other's best worst jest. That is when life was undressed. Reminiscing and learning, a deeper connection blooming. With you by my side, nothing seemed looming, only a test.

When I'd get glimpses of who you were, not who you thought everyone did. When stares were electric and piercing, a moment when egos slid out the window and emotions poured fiercely.

Alas, it's true, sometimes it's all I do, just sit missing yo

How to Deserve a Partner in Mind

Act valiantly and not gallantly. In yourself feel
proudly but do not speak loudly. Be carefree but
caring, also be a bit daring. Impress their parents,
especially if they dislike them, but always be on
their right with them. You can't be pushy or act
too obscene. Say only words you truly mean.

Read their mood but not their status; be handy
with some apparatus. Give them space—no one
likes being chased. Unless they do? Then maybe
become famous for using Kung Fu? Or saving
them from danger, but here's the hanger. You
would never wish harm even on a stranger.

It's all so easy to do in my mind, yet fortune
remains unkind. These situations all are so
contrived. I wish I could do it in real life.

Existence shows there is only one test, for us to
do our best. The rest is out of our hands. We
must but try and meet love's demands.

Fishes

As life flows, I try not to be too resistant, sucked into its depth with a persistent pull, so much excitement leading to a lull. Seeing stripes and spots sitting in a chair. Knowing where I am but feeling completely lost. Feeding on pearls of thought as my mind is awhirl grasping with fingers frail. Hoping for relief in medicine measured on scales.

The pain stabs and throbs as the needle jabs and robs me of life's essence. All in search of some self-presence. The doctor wants preservation but so far, I have my reservations. More pills to correct what nature made, all for a life everyone but me wants to save.

It's better to have loved and lost. Sure, but that doesn't mean I enjoy the cost. I tumble through life's tide. Doing my best to enjoy the ride, but I can no longer see the light above. Floating and swimming through muffled sound. Trying to find which way is up. The answer is never at the bottom of a cup. Though it does numb the pain and help me forget the cause of the latest numbing eruption. As the pull of my emotions have such strong suction. I feel nailed to the floor.

Sick fish whirl around in circles, but I swirl in verticals of emotion. Up and down, so much so, I'm not exactly a pleasure to be around.

My arms grow weary of paddling, even a child's screams of joy are addling. Through so many emotions surrounding me I seek simple grounding. In hopes that I can resist the pull and gain a fish's short memory, one not so disturbed by the sensory.

Halloween Spooktacular

With a jaundiced eye unsteadily, he stands.
The man rubs his parchment-like hands over his
paunch. O' he looks like he's six months
pregnant in his dirty ripped poncho. He licks his
lips and salutes an American banner hanging
from the back of an old bronco, lifted like a
Tonka.

The light flips green. We've all seen it. The man
spits on him as he goes past.

I introduce Dan Duke, Private First Class. He
served two tours in Southern Afghanistan. When
he was the undisputed last man standing near a
three-meter crater that got made by accident.

He wipes the spittle off his face in a haze of coal,
the smell of diesel and burnt rubber deep in his
nose. He flexes his calloused toes as a patriot
rolls down their window and tells him to "stop
freebootin" as if he'd been looting much more
than their time. If he's ever caught standing in
their sight.

The price of fighting for others' freedom.
In this newest kingdom and colonial empire.
You see it's cheaper and more accessible to
drown in Porter's Fire than catch a bus for an
hour or five to the nearest VA. He just needs a
place to lay. After another day of pangs of
hunger and hearing the thunder of guns ravage
his mind. Next to a detonated mine that only he
survived.

To fight and to serve is a hell of a price to pay in
the good ol' US of A. It's too high a tariff.
It's cheaper to have more sheriffs who assault the
homeless for salary, hiding behind a thin blue
line.

We only pay prisoners hourly. Punishing Dan for
the crime of coming home. Everybody knows a
casket gets more votes.

Dan turns swiping the air and yells. Shying away
from the sound of shells only he can hear.
Ain't it swell? He's stuck in hell so we can secure
the value of the dollar bill to capitalist-made
perils in the cradle of humanity. We justify it
with such vanity.

Don't worry. He will probably freeze to death
tonight.
One less person in the food line.
One more casket on Newsline.

Beloved American hero "John Duke" was found
dead on the side of the road.

"This is a travesty," said the men in power with
stern-faced glowers as they sold weapons to
drug dealers and stopped testing with LSD.

We can only solve this problem next November
at the booths. It's the same line since Babe Ruth.
All I can tell you is Dan's Truth. It's too late to
wait. We've already failed. Happy Halloween.
This shit is real.

Fragments

The Universe makes more sense when you realize God created us in their image. Broken.

A child abuser so forlorn by their mistakes they slaughtered their firstborn. Somehow this is supposed to be an inspiring token.

A voice so grand and profound they communicate as an inflamed bush on the ground. Behold all, the brushfire has spoken.

Creating creatures obsessed with progressing their score. Regardless of its impact on humanity's core. It's fine as long as they donate 10% or more to the folks in power.
I thought God's son came back and that part was reformed. Oh, it's just the bits you didn't care for? So much for turning the other cheek.

It's alright, we are human; our opinions change by the week. For some by the hour. In ways we rarely choose to seek. It's funny how that greed tends to creep.

The price is steep if you decided to believe in yourself instead of your elders, the bourgeoise who told us we should never be welders then refuse to be sellers without their hard-earned profit. All in the name of their tacked-up prophet.

Ridiculing our need to be recognized by the generations who specialized in giving their kids awards. To brag about in the board room after they finished stashing tax dollars offshore. When they paid for college working part-time and nothing more.

Money, like faith, is an illusion. They use when a situation needs diffusing. The damage that's done by the lawless braless. Covered in masks as our parents blast us with tear gas. For having the audacity for chanting "I can't breathe" but have you considered the revenue lost? When they shut down a fast-food joint, slinging ravaged beef.

We all love the police until they attack what we view as free, this armed militia providing capitalist security. Shooting handcuffed men in the streets. We can't judge that. What was the suspect like when he was three?

We should be surprised that the nation once on the rise worships police. Because they worship a guy the cops nailed to a tree, and have never read past John 3.

Culturally frenetic, we judge people for what's genetic. Then refuse to use antiseptic during a pandemic. Incapable of wholistic thought, science races and our humanity lies stagnant. We should put more trust in management, but what the hell do I know? I'm just a fragment of a being, trying to justify all around me what I keep seeing.

Thinking, While Drinking

Every day it rings true, when I feel the sunshine,
I think of you. The chill in my bones sings
through. The warmth I need when alone is aloof.

Every day this hole sinks deeper, but they can't
put a ceiling on my feelings. When I look above, I
see those rays and I can't be fazed. Like stars in
the sky, you shine brightest in the dark.
You need not worry, daylight is but an illusion
brought on by the lark. Stars do shine just as
brightly at noon, it's simply the night sky
illumined.

I don't care about being righteous, I'm always
going to fight for this. Though fate like the planet
may spin you away. I hope eventually I'll be
wrapped back in your rays.

There's something to be said for coincidental
timing, is this just our stars aligning?
The thought has me singing, flinging my soul
into the universe. All of these people at the bar
are cringing.

The man with a ponytail said it's time for me to be leaving. I'm just coping with my bereavement. The barman is just hoping I'll leave a tip.

Wiping myself off from sliding on the ground. I want to tell you something profound. I want you to feel surrounded by universal love. Hugging you tightly like a glove. It's okay if I'm not in your bubble or your legs have stubble. I love that you're a rebel, I want to experience your revelation. When you have the sensation of universal creation. Your star shining brightest when the eclipse is lifted in jubilation.

Words seem flaccid and far too passive; I want your world lit up like you're on acid and take you on the best trip of your life. If I could, I would eat all your strife and pain so you could feel whole again.

To help you realize that like the sun you're more than just your sum. Your radiance transcends galaxies. I don't want you to think this fallacy. I would build you a palace free of charge. I want to say this passively. I don't want to sell you on anything but the truth. I would do anything for you.

Alas, I've cast myself into Limbo.

For fear of sin, though I've relived every word
and thought a thousand times. I feel banished,
unaware of crimes I've committed. So this poem
will live remitted to a love unrequited. Our
future lies omitted.

Maybe one day our stars will come into phase
and align. Then I will feel your beautiful light
shine. Until then, I'll stumble through this
lifetime.

Purpose

What if our soul's purpose is to return our experiences back to that light? To a universal consciousness when we one day die. The existence of all, on its evolutionary crawl.

Therefore, our purpose is to give life more depth than its surface.

I've tried to live my life for others and was smothered by my lack of self. I don't know how to be anyone else.

So if I have my druthers, I'll be the best me that I can be. One that lets myself be free to feel, and love. To hell with all that other stuff.

I've had my life flash before my eyes. Six, seven, or eight times. Each instance I barely wanted to keep trying. I've decided I'll do what it takes if I'm going to report back on my expiration date, I can say, "Life? ...it was pretty fucking great."

Dropping Anchor

I'm surrounded by transcendent beauty; the
grass is green, and the trees are changing.
There's a soft breeze, but it isn't getting through
to me. I wish I could say something moving, but
the words elude me.

I just feel an anxious pull as if there's a gap in my
chest. That's where calmness should rest.

Since the incident, it's left me bereft of so many
feelings and emotions. Enough sorrow to fill
oceans, firm ideas have become notions.

Unfortunately, big impacts have precedent,
however I've never experienced this tactic. My
stomach is full of acid, the aches are blasting,
constantly my emotions are just die in the
casting.

I'm praying for contentment but it's just sixes.
What's in my drink? I can't remember what I
mixed in.

Oh yeah, there's a system of calming. I notice the pink in the sky pawing against the grey. As we make it through another day.

I can feel a breeze on my lips as I take a deep breath, moving down through my sternum. This part is most germane, that I remain sane. As I feel the ground through my shoes and weather these blues.

My fingers tap as I make another poem. Smelling the chill air and a hint of loam. I may not see Aphrodite on a shell caressed in foam, but at least I'm living in this week's home.

Storms batter my sails as I cling to the rails, but when I feel insanity's rancor, I simply must remember to drop anchor.

Mountain Valley

The frost in the grass leaves a path as you walk past, another of dawn's long shadows. The light is grey with hints of orange coming through the haze of clouds. Rays of light flickering through leaves like a freshly lit tallow.

The air is clean, and you can see the wagging tail of your companion. Wandering farther, you see a misty canyon. A path of cobblestones and soft luminescence, a feeling of the perfect temperature wraps around your presence. You see a lily come to life in a searing ray of sunlight. A drop of dew presents itself upon the nearest petal. With outstretched fingers you caress it lightly. The temptation challenging your metal.

Brushing your fingers across your lips, you feel the dew spread across the skin. Like a bit of frost. A feeling spreads, a soft press on your bosom. Your thoughts become lofty, freed of their chained prison. The feeling remains hotly but the memories silently vanish. It's as if you knew the story, not in English but in Spanish.

You walk the path and upon the walls, your
favorite memories display and you feel their call.
Your favorite tale about an adventurous steward.
In every way it's like your first time through it.
Except one feeling has clung. Your love for this
has not just begun. Built in years of loving
reflection. That is the flavor of your new life's
direction.

To have experienced the flavor but once would
sate the thirst with little fuss. Though if ever
again the sun presents to me. The chance to see, a
fire-born lily.

I know one simple truth: before me lies the soft
caress and joyous proof, of my soul's fountain of
youth.

Heavy

It's probably best I tell people I'm fine.
Considering I constantly regret not dying. When
you carry so much weight it's trying, it's not fair
to everyone else keeping an eye on you.

There is this weird feeling to knowing death.
Once you embrace it, like concrete it's set.
Sometimes I can feel it coming and honestly, I'm
not sure which way I should be running. The
responsible part of my brain knows the right
answer, but its lack of reasons is stunning.

Everyone will miss me? Sure, a few people
might. But that reasoning isn't super tight.
Honestly, I'm scared, dying is easy, and
happiness is scarce. I get hung up on the
dumbest shit, I know I'll get through it, but the
despair is so real. Sometimes it's all I can feel.

Better to put on some music and take Poppy for a
drive. It's another day I can check the box
without a lie. When people ask how I'm doing, I
can say, "Alive." I know it makes people
unsteady, but lately all I feel is heavy.

SAM

Driving over another dusty pass. You're driving
too damn fast. You can run from a lot of things,
but never from your past.

Caught on your shoulders like a tattered cape.
You do your best to just behave, but some stains
remain. No matter how big your smile, you're
being crushed by the strain.

Skidding around corners your knuckles are
white. The car you pass flips around as you see
the lights. It's okay, you were never coming
home tonight.

It doesn't really matter since your reality was
shattered. The fields below lay in scattered
eastern shadows. You're driving back through
heartbreak as the tires shake through the next
turn.

Driving past houses with three-car garages, the
farms are slowly becoming mirages. This town's
changed almost as much as you. Out here on the
fringes, the roar of the engines screams through.

The windows are down and there is a foot of snow on the ground as the sweat mixes in with your silent tears. Is it the living or the dying that you fear? Knowing now that she will never be near.

You might just beat the sunset to the park. As you fly through the four-way stop. Skidding into the lot, the car slightly rocks as you fling open the door into the stark cold.

You just want to swing there once more behind that barn. There is cold blood running down your arm. It sounds like you're in a tunnel as you hear a shout. You glance back, and the sheriff has his gun out.

With a crack and a flash, you twist like a marionette lifted off the ground. The snow feels like ash as your back smashes into a snowy mound.

You clutch the crumpled stained note in your hand. As tattooed arms grope through your pockets. The man swears and checks your pulse. As your eyes roll back into their sockets. Seeing the alpenglow before you take a last stroll through memories. It lasts but a moment, but it feels like centuries.

After your last rattling gasp, the officer notices the note you clasped. He struggles with cold clutching fingers until you release your grasp. Your body just got slightly lighter as your soul takes flight o'er the grizzly scene.

The cop realizing he has just murdered an intended suicide victim. Now he will have to file a report in the system. About how he shot an unarmed man for speeding and fleeing to the scene of a man's favorite dream.

The last place he saw her laugh. Before the long slow beep on the machine.

Gone

Careening through my heart and mind, I don't know how I'm going to find it. The answer to the questions deep inside.

Another week without clarity, as I try to feel my way home. The reflection just keeps staring back at me. It's just too damn long to be alone. I'll keep on waiting for an infinity if I just had a sign given to me. Without it, the path just has so many steps. I know it's a lot to ask for you to deal with me. The weight just makes me feel so much more stress.

The smell of cold, and the bump from the cigarettes. You can't stand that I knew what it was from. I wish I was still cursed with forgetfulness, that way I'd still feel numb. Gone, so close but too far to reach. It doesn't matter how hard I seek. Gone is all you'll ever be.

Love is for a lifetime, even when it changes. You're just out of my sight line, hearing a different language.

You might as well be a million miles away. Maybe I'll see you in my dreams tonight, that's the only place you're willing to stay the night.

Now I aimlessly wander over yonder hills and prairies. Seeking cures of metaphysical abnormalities. Probably standing in an unseen line of patients waiting patiently. Nursing heart aches and needing pity, looking for your loving sympathy, to heal them of their crimes. Forgiveness is all we've wanted our entire lifetime.

Every time I have a moment to think. My heart grows then starts to shrink. This foundation's burnt and starting to creak.

Gone, so close but too far to reach. It doesn't matter how hard I seek. Gone is all you'll ever be.

Gone, so close but too far to reach. It doesn't matter how hard I seek.

Gone is all you'll ever be. To me...

Curiosity

I guess I'm just another cat, because I'm honestly
baffled. If every relationship, we have had is flat.
Then why not run back to our one castle?

The one pinnacle where the disaster we met was
after we fled. For a few months, I never wished I
was dead. All of this makes sense in my head.
The problem is in solace, there's not many
options to be said.

I'm sitting here unraveling all the strings of
memories and possibilities. It's like being lost in
a foreign country, trying to understand which
street I'm on.
Clutching at straws with rough scarred claws,
while being consumed in cruelty's maw.
Was it interest that I saw?
From that which once was lost?
It's a knot I run into often.

I want to slip outside of my trends and habits.
Glaring just outside the bounds of this cabin.

Staring into the distance imagining a place
where:
I.
Am.
Free.
One unbound by this curiosity, but what if it's
not the heaven that I seek?

Searching

I keep looking for you everywhere I go. This feeling deep inside of me knows you'll never show. Roving miles for the sight of you across the dirt and snow.

I drive these places so that even when I'm lost. An impression lies behind me, reminding me of the cost. Random chance and poor decisions lay on the ground where tossed. Covered in two feet of powdery frost.

I keep digging and kicking, trying to find them again. Tears and terror struggling to escape from deep within. I just want to see my old best friend. The one who made my spirit soar like the freeborn wind.

Stranded in a parking lot, stuck in two feet of snow. It would be so easy to just quit, but deep inside I know. The struggle will be worth it If I always trust my nose. Every good story has a few frost-bitten toes.

I'll just keep on groping for some semblance of meaning. The freezing cold is all a bit deceiving. My heart's racing in my chest, as I keep doing what I do best. Scraping and clawing without rest. If I'm being honest, I'd rather freeze to death.

Instead, I'm covered in sweat, digging with frozen fingers in a vest. I may not be a winner, but I'll never quit. Even if you can't feel it anymore, you'll always be worth it.

Even if I never see you again, I won't give up on you. I'll always love you deep within. I'll always keep searching.

Send It

Boy, you've thought enough. Give it all you've got, for love. It's the moment where you rise or fall. You'll never know what happens until you see what you've bought.

Your ass keeps cashing checks you hope this one clears. Some people are born with the credit for that to never be a fear. It's the moment where you sit back and let fate steer. You've done everything it takes to get here.

It's the leap of faith, you've done it hundreds of times before. Don't speed-check, you'll come up short. Every time you try and be sly and control the uncontrollable, you risk dying. Hearts have stopped, brains have broken, all in search of a token.

Nothing tangible but what's barely imaginable. That feeling of wholly feeling glory so holy it's your sole existence's purpose. You've committed, you can't reverse this.

Onwards! To where heroes are made and souls are saved. That existential moment where we but glimpse our graves.

Morning Coffee

The sunrise comes up over snowcapped
mountains. Clouds drifting across those jagged
peaks. Standing in front of me is a homeless
person fighting a memory only they can see.

The air is brisk and cold. A plume of breath
escapes every time he screams. Arms held in
front of him for a fight he doesn't want, that bit's
clear to me. The terror in his eyes, but he's too
proud to flee.

Everyone is watching but doesn't want to be
seen, some of us are worried, others think it's
funny. Just another day in American society.

Deepest Secrets

Trigger warning Scenes of violence, suicide, and sexual abuse portrayed.

When I get embarrassed, I wish I could hit myself with a hammer. I'm not much for suicide, you need to be a planner. That's not the way I want to be a person of note. I guess it's better to be a man of letters, just breathe and realize that no one hates me would be even better.

I must always deflect with jests, to keep others' potential rage in check. In my mind I know it's ridiculous, but my mother's training was meticulous. I must anticipate what might be coming so I can be calming; these silences are alarming. It's time to be charming.

No one can know that deep inside, I'm a neglected child. Screaming for help when there's no food on the shelf because Mom is tired.

The laundry room is defined by piles.
She had to stay up all night rearranging all her shit. So she can't remember where she put it.

It's alright if the shelf isn't stocked. Dad's at work and you can just walk two miles to eat free hot dogs and mini drinks. That will cost thousands of dollars for a shrink to reconstruct. So I can deconstruct why I am so easily beguiled to do what others think.

Let's dive deep if I want to survive. How about that time I was molested when I was five.

Lurking at the public library. Like myself, he wasn't sure what to choose.

He went for just another random selection. I was very confused to be used by a man with a mustache. Passing his avalanche of self-hatred onto a random boy looking for a story, but one a bit more boring.

That I don't have to be storing so deep inside. It's not for polite conversation. A young boy's minor molestation.

There was that other time when I was nine and surprised by a trusted one's lies. That it's important to just practice kissing and being rubbed. So now I can't help but want to be

scrubbed with hot water, and barbed wire.
Because some poor child passed on what
happened from their bastard father.

Nothing quite like being a grown man and
getting uncomfortable if someone is too closely
standing. Just constantly wondering if he's going
to try and kiss me. Maybe it's ego and I think he
can't resist me. The truth, is I'm living in constant
terror from a person's social error. At least
recently bubbles have been expanding.

Maybe it was the sibling standing on my chest in
the pond, water up to his elbows as I was
floundering underneath him screaming that I'm
drowning. Then a few years later he's sitting on
my chest pounding me on the forehead with his
favorite ring. That way I would grow up and be
tough. It's really heart-warming stuff.

I don't know how to stop loving and caring. The
evidence is glaring. I'm so used to being
abandoned for reasons increasingly random that
most of my memories, I can't stand them.

Rainy Days

The rain feeds my soul like it feeds the ground, the vibrant colors, the muted sounds. The ripple on the roof as I cruise around through the mountains.

The wipers sway, pushing away blurred thoughts. Doesn't matter where I'm headed. I know where I'd rather be; it's feelings that are sought. To feel love and purpose deeper than on the surface. Sometimes, going for a drive is all I've got.

Turning down new roads and finding old ruts. Sometimes, the deepest paths are the ones you should trust. Looking for more than just street signs. The roll of gravel is comforting as it dulls out the sounds of my mind.

I just want to roll; not so many starts and stops. This road has made too many broken hearts. I wish this rain could give me a fresh start.

Friends

I will always love you from my peak until I'm
absorbed into the land. I'll never know what I
did, but somehow you welcomed me into your
family. The one with choices, the one that's
actually planned.

I've wandered my whole life, roaming from band
to band of like-minded fans. I don't always click
in; some people just don't understand.

I don't know how to feel anymore; not that I
don't have emotions. Just ones so strong I can
barely stand. They come like waves in the ocean,
more than enough for any man.

I'm lucky to have you, accepted as I am. Lifting
me up when I don't give a damn.

Life can be terrible, filled with horrible stuff.
You're the ones who remind me that I am
enough.

Snuggle

For the first time, the thought of a noose seemed
comforting. A snug little scarf with a little sting.
These thoughts come randomly; my brain is
choking. My wit's diseased. That's all these
things mean.

I've been to the edge and looked death full on. It
doesn't have eyes or teeth just blackness that
goes wrong.

The terror that grips behind your clavicle, it's
your hope going on sabbatical.

The absolute certainty that you're being ripped
into that black hole. It takes every ounce of
willpower as it grips at your throat.

You grasp and rip at your energies thread. Just to
escape the moment of death. Here's the thing,
though: Death is patient.

You'll be reporting back to your previous station.
Death is the lover that will always embrace you,
no matter your story it will devastate you.

Gobbling you up in its giant black maw. It's not greedy. It's just nature's law. Nothing to be scared of, it's not death's fault. There's no need to force it—there, my friend, is the art.

When you find yourself at this finish line, turn around. There are new truths to mine. To live and enjoy as much as you can. By helping others and continuing to stand.

Owning your center and looking to give, this can be your new purpose to live.

Find those things that you wish you could change and do them again until your regrets no longer remain. Everyone in your life is a placeholder for your story. This time, make a life surrounded by glories.

I can tell you this single truth: You're not starting over. You've got your life's knowledge inside of you. Use it to make a better world not just for me, but you. I promise you, I will too.

Pressure

It comes in many forms and often disarms. The incredible force of the universe guiding us this way and that. Life is a test; as we rise, we are crushed flat.

Striving for happiness and self-love I feel like life's heels are crushing the back of my skull, as I'm biting into a curb. Some of the pressure is my own creation, but I'm not responsible for all the degradation.

My state of being is crushed, my senses are overly flushed with the forces of space. Heat and cold, lack of air and at perceived risk of heavenly calamity.

I just want to be free; this feeling is so overwhelming. Trying to keep my head above water, I'm afraid of drowning those around me.

I need the peace of grounding, but one can never step outside of space to view the universe. We always feel pressure's curse.

I seek the reinforcement of kindness and being
wanted. Those traits that are so vaunted.

I love you all.
I promise, I'm trying my best.
I just need fate to let me catch my breath.

Youth

An enigmatic truth, the wounds of our youth.
Most unintended, rarely mended.
Oft contended.

These seemingly innocent slights that strike right
to one's core.
I am not all that you say.
I am so much more!
We scream from inside.
Our energy ruminating through the sky.

Different is not wrong; not knowing a bird does
not change the beauty of its song.
The world does not know me, how can you?
I am a creature of my own making.
If not design, I will not be tamed, I will be free
and wild.

Our youth is our time of growth, to be nurtured.
Not contrived to live your passion-filled lies.
As a child I lost my voice from screaming at
night, trying to be heard and seen.
My own personal being,
not your gingerbread thing.

Too kneaded and without proving.
My stride was beaten, not my own choosing.
Now I must decide who I am to be in this life.
The person you made died.

Pain

I've spent my life living in pain, so engrossed I often didn't complain. The direct cause did not always get named.

My mantra was: *C'est la vie*. Living life complacently.

I should have been better at mentioning it, instead I just carried on resenting it.
Suffering in silence. Like Job, living through a myopic lens. Hurting all around me in my efforts to help. All because I lost my sense of self.

Through the revelation of sharing my experiences. I've learned I can stop fearing it. While pain is something that you cannot lose. Here is a secret: There is pain you can choose.

Escape the pain of self-doubt by looking for a new climbing route. To choose one's pain allows us to embrace adventure's name.

What if your suffering is self-flagellation, a construct of your own imagination?

In your mind's eye. Imagine looking in a mirror. It's your favorite room behind you. The image is crisp and clear.

What do you see? Turn around, now what do you perceive? One is a life with you, one without. The only difference is perspective's shout.

Embrace this moment, and realize no matter how hard you've tried, your story is also on the other side. Live your favorite dream from this moment on. The struggles will be there, but this decision will lead you on.

Choose the pain that brings you hope and joy despite the risk. All that's required is a new perspective.

This could be the end, or a magnificent new beginning of something you've never imagined. A life filled with pains and passions of your choice.

It's up to you.
Shall we mourn? Or rejoice?

Anguish

I sometimes wonder if I'm addicted to pain and anguish and too big a coward to face it.

The fear of causing any for someone I hold dear is apocalyptic. My soul's portrait would be revered in cryptic triptych.

It's the deep-seated knowledge that you know the pain of giving too much. Watching while everything around you crumbles to dust.

At some point, it's self-manifested.
I learned that by sitting on holy oak benches.
Staring at a person I was led to believe gave the greatest sacrifice for me. So I could even have the opportunity for a paradisiacal delivery.

Ahh, the chivalry.

I was taught only to give in order to deserve true love. Sometimes, the pain is just too much...

Or…

Maybe it's the anguish. Traits held only by the
famous; at least that is how fate arranged it. It's
not just genetics, it's how we've raised them.
Parents working 40-hour weeks to get a bank
statement. Reflecting the value of their lives.
Force to make children survive.

On.
Their.
Own.

It doesn't matter the size of your home, just
throw them in the cartoon zone. I have a lot of
voices, I'm not sure which is truly my own. I'm
trying to ease it by writing these poorly formed
poems.

This deep eternal anguish, it's hard to erase it.

Dig in and breathe.

You and I've got this for as long as we can. I may
not know you, but I can understand.

Keep it gritty, try and be witty, breathe in. Fill in your deep energy. Focus it on something you trust.

It's hard to hear it, but we only exist due to universal luck and quantum physics.

Which means that while we didn't always control what brought us here, from this moment forward, we choose what happens. You are strong enough to make the tough choice and tell your story with your voice.

I know, the heart tremors just to think it. It's more than you can wish, but it is possible to live without constant anguish.

So Close

The universe is so infinitely improbable. Yet here I sit with a problem that is unsolvable. The ability and arrogance to imagine a different life. One with less sorrow and strife.

One where my dreams reside, not as thoughts of my unconscious mind. One where you are next to me, sharing a life. That goes on, much like this one. Except we felt like we belonged, and there were no concerns of someone feeling wronged.

A universe where we both exist in joy and happiness. Is that too much to propose? A life that glows when we are close.

Dream So Good

Do you ever have a dream, one that's so perfect you know its meaning instantly? If you're lucky, you can recall that vignette consistently.

It feels so real, making my heart ache. I can feel your smile, your perfect eyes surprising me with delight. Your shy way of acknowledging maybe it was fate.

This dream is a past reality, lost in greatest calamity. Roads of fate wind and roll, maybe ours will intertwine when the time is right for our souls.

Until then, I can simply sit and reminisce for that which I so greatly miss. To have these memories is a gift. It's understood that I'm blessed to have a dream so good.

This Moment

A volcanic explosion defined by emotion,
enhancing your talent quotient. The smells. the
sounds, the touch. It's the perfect amount, you
have enough

An instant so infinitely large and infinitesimally
small, it has more power than a lepton's pull.
This magic experience deep in your soul,
solidifying your being into something pure,
answering life's muteness with an effervescent
lure.

When life is strenuous or feeling dull, the
absurdity of joy is when I feel full.

Death

Dear Death,

Sweet, beautiful Death, how I've longed to give you my last breath. I have wronged you in your loving grasp.

Alas, I'm doing it again. You thought you had me, but I'm staying. I've decided to strain through the pain. Resist your lusty refrain.

I would feel too guilty to willfully toss you a life not skillfully embossed with joy and adventure.

I will put in more effort than Rasputin in a tracksuit. Our dispute has history. You know I have always been confounded by your mysterious nature of overwhelming greed and that supercilious stature. Luring us all to your dinner party.

Sitting alone feasting on our souls' experiences, screaming like a toddler starting to devour ice cream. I have given you plenty to seize around me. Loved ones, friends, and family.

One day you'll attain me dressed scantily, giving way to your seduction frantically. When I've truly had enough positive moments steering my senses to return. Calling to the heavens, "I'm done with my turn."

I will have lived my life to the fullest as I creakily swan dive down your gullet.

Experience my life as the light shines through when I join the universal truth of energy. No longer fearing you as an enemy, but as the repository of my life's loves and passions. To be in your embrace everlasting.

With the greatest love and respect, let's continue this game of chess until my last aged breath.

Love,
Weston
11/30/2022

About the Author

Weston Charlesworth lives with his dog and all-around best friend, Poppy. They love to see new things and listen to music together. You can often see them out ski touring or biking in the mountains near their home. Following a series of traumatic events that culminated in being struck by a car on his bike in 2022, Weston began writing poetry to cope with the dissociation and CPTSD episodes triggered by that event. The poems contained in this book were written between September and November of 2022. He is an adamant supporter of mental health awareness.